RIPPLES OF HEART

AN ANTHOLOGY OF POEMS

RAMESH CHANDRA PRADHANI

ISBN 979-888546491-8

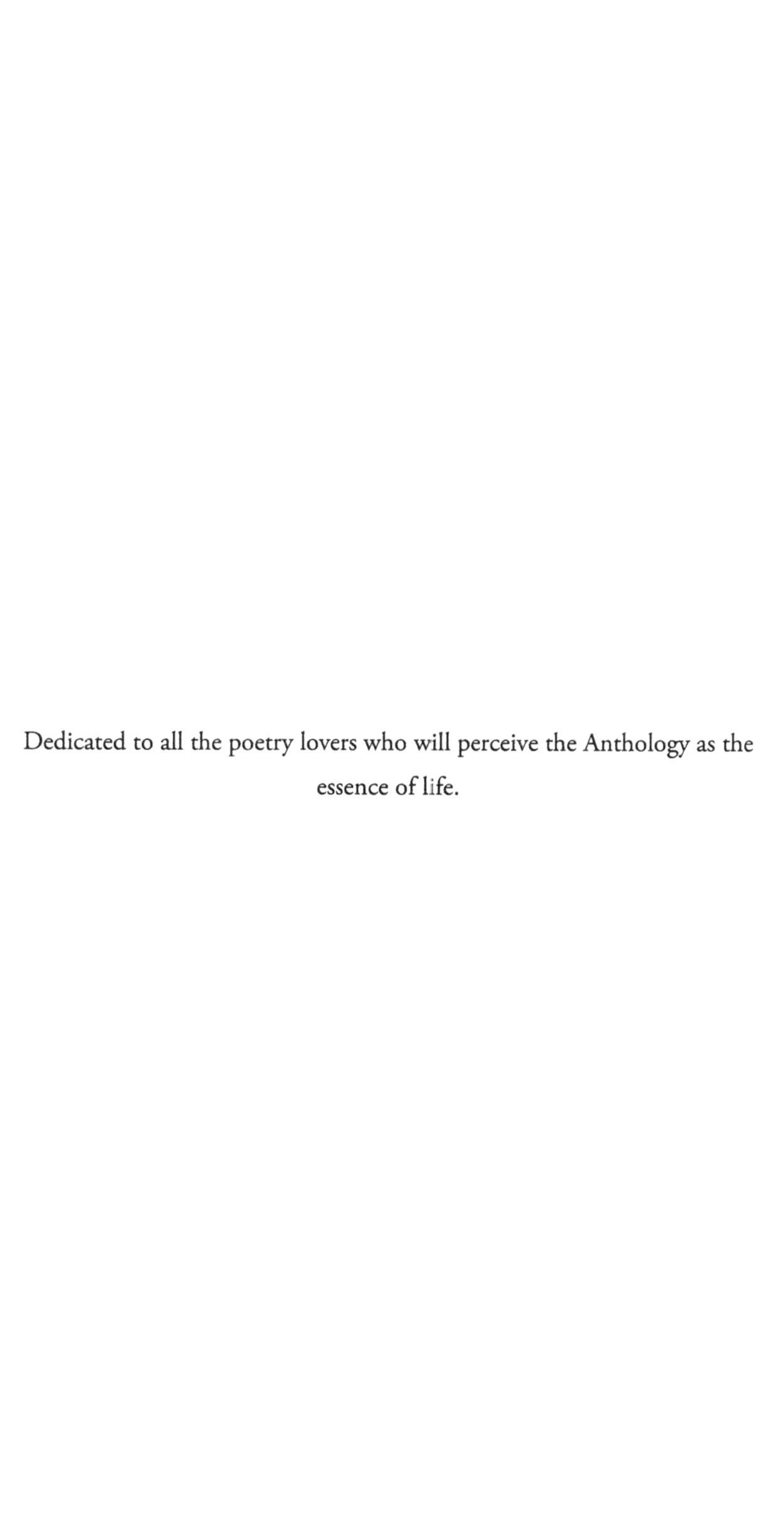

Dedicated to all the poetry lovers who will perceive the Anthology as the essence of life.

Contents

Contents

Contents

Contents

Contents

Preface

Poetry is the sum total of the artistic expression of life, no matter bad or good. A painter paints the picture in lively and moving manner to allure the attention of the onlookers, likewise a poet draws and colours the words sometimes with the sweetness or bitterness of past memories or the feelings and emotions in the form of poetry garnering from day to day happenings experiencing circumstances occuring all around . Each poem is the reflection of the poet's personal or impersonal intuition that makes the poet sanguine of searching the newness of creation inking in his own way of perception. It is poetry that makes one laugh and cry and warns the repercussion to guide oneself on the way of life's journey enriching with heightened sensibility ,unfathomable hope and incredible faith.

Most of the poems in this Anthology are based upon the various facets of life exploring the signifuicance of love, peace, unity, divine bliss, courage, confidence ,tolerance, success, failure and many more. Needless to mention that each poem in this work is a lamp post to illuminate the path of complexity and hopelessness and acts as a panacea to sphysical and mental anguish. The thoughts intertwined in the poems might unfurl the umbrella in the rain, blanken in the winter and the shield to protect against the thunderbolt of distressing life.

Ramesh Chandra Pradhani

Acknowledgements

I am humbly grateful to the Almighty for His benign grace behind the completion of this work. I am also highly thankful to thewhole team of Notion Press for publishing the Anthology in due time. The moral support of my family members in bringing out the publication is of immense praise.

Ramesh Chandra Pradhani

1. Different Colours One World

Different colours make a rainbow in the sky
Different stars in moonlit hide faces being shy
Different races make a society gregarious
Mankind is their only identity
Different people speak different language for the same expression
Different people from different culture and heritage drives for unification
Different creepers trees and bushes make a lovely forest purposeful
Human mind the deep and dark density arrest so forgetful
Different rivers from different places make an ocean worldwide
Water where remains in still motion unfathomable teaching mankind
Diversity brings unity the powerful culture
Unity holds diversity of places, things color.
Difference the law of nature inevitable
To balance the creation more suitable.
Difference differs however a world of difference
But under one umbrella we are all with many a preference.

2. Mother and Child

Mother and child a sacred union inseparable
No mighty power segregate not at all capable.
Two sides of the same coin
Union of them is a boon
Mother and child like body and head God's creation
How can you divide divine combination.
Mother child union, the union of body and blood
Union of milk and water
Union of life and soul
Union of shadow and pole
One is eye the other eye doll
Union of water and fish
How can you sunder water
By the blow of a stick.
Two legs of a compass
Two wheels of a cart
Tied with the knot of axle of love
The bridge between mother and child
Erected on the pillars divine.
Indestructible the union of mother and child
Unmeasurable the depth of relation
Child the disciple mother is the guide
Sacred, palpable, immortal unison.

3. If you want something Change

Melt like snow to wash away your self
Flow like river to mingle with others to help
Blow like wind to access each entrance
Bloom like flowers to give away fragrance
Dream like a dreamer to achieve success
Live like a bagger to dream nothingness
Love like a mother to have no condition
Sleep like a dog to know the unknown
Focus like an intent heron not to miss a chance
Bathe like a crow to reach the target in advance
Be like the blind to suppress egoistic sense
Be the brake of your life to save your present existence
Be a child the image of God to avoid vanity and pride
Be the colourful light to make the milieu bright inside and outside
Be the spring of humanity to enrich mankind with peace and prosperity
Be the cuckoo of life to mesmerise the solitary to rejoice tranquility
Be like a candle to dedicate all you have for other benevolence
Be the rising sun of hope to instill patience with full confidence
Be the song to cheer every life with one's value and depth
Be the cultivator to sow the seeds in the land of heart good will and faith.
If you want to change do something instead of nothing
Slowly and steadily change will come to everything.

4. Sparkle like a Diamond

Open heart expression
Feelings and emotions
Whisper your adoration
Years of consolation
O sweet my sweet heart
Sparkle like diamond inside
Preserved with great heed
That really lightened my mind.
O Diamond of my heart
I know you never depart
Silent just to take part
In deep love comfort
Wherever you are or were
Wherever will you be there
None can hide you within
You are mine what I mean.
Worried not about you
You are my unfaded hue
Sparkle like diamond
As long as exit the world.
Our love, I am sure, diamond like pure
Let time fly and flee away
But love never let us go astraya

5. Unforgetful Childhood

Unforgetful memories are childhood days
Some sweet some bitter
Still remain untold without having a privilege
Now is the time to express better.
The moment of joy and freedom
Absent in the register of my life's dictum.
Far away from the madding crowd
No voice I had to speak what I wished loud
The flower of my life about to fade away
But my future I think consoled me not to go astray
Pretentions was a companion to me all the long
Who hid me inside from the reality before the throng
Sipping air quenching my thirst and hunger
Sumptuous food I dreamt no longer
Sometimes water was bread and butter
Thanks to the Almighty for the gift of nature
Amidst the crush of childhood I stood
Thy poverty being assumed as daily food
Now what I am the sole blessings of His kind grace
But for Him life would be an accursed mess.

6. React With No Reaction

Though every action has reaction
But react not with any reaction
When there's no situation
No demand of attention
Except self consolation
React not with any reaction
When Time stops Motion
Speechless is Commotion
Silence has no exception
Wise to avoid botheration.
Often unnecessary reaction
Leads to unhealthy situation
Pushing into awkward position
Might provoke indelible tension.
But silence gives consent
To accept what prevalent
Be eyewitness to injustice
Running away from justice
Think to be silent or violent
It's our absolute choice

7. Love And Lust

Love is eternal a divine gift
A two ways faithful communication
Lust is ephemeral and sinful act
Invites own destruction
Love is reciprocal, mutual and perpetual
Two sides of affectionate interaction
Lust is personal, partial and unsocial
Unrequited unhealthy situation
Love moulds character and broadens mind scope
A sense of understanding adjustment compromise and cooperation
Lust loses character and cuts the rope of hope.
A transitory moment of selfishness and molestation
Love reforms, transforms and reshapes
Creating miraculous record break history
Lust deforms, defames, and defaces
Values of human life
Love refills, relives and refines
Something in a novel way
Lust hinders, sunders and defiles
Everything letting go astray
Love is sharing, caring, nurturing and rapturing
Near and dear without differentiating
Lust is panic, smearing, and disgusting
Contagion in infecting, affecting
Love is feeling, liking, and forgiving

Selfless devotion assured commitment
Lust is heartless, careless and detesting
Expectations in return reverie in fulfilment
Love is life, light and birth
Hope for the hopeless for cheerless mirth
Lust is dark, lifeless and death
Spirit of evils, a pool of sin, of humanity dearth.

8. Life And Morality

Life without morality is painting without colour
Seeds of morality germinated life born ever
Life a budding flower morality it's fragrance
No perfume spreads unless it blooms in stance
Morality makes man humbler and nobler
Grows gently, steadily life it's holder
Life gets reshaped, refined and moulded for good
With the presence of morality like nourishing food
Life without morality a horse without reign
Equally uncontrolled if failed to tame
Life demonstrated everywhere blissful
With morality it proved meaningful
Everything useless unless purpose served
Otherwise may take to unwanted curved
Where there is life there is morality
Lacking of morality lacking of humanity
Good deeds make men moral beings
Bad one invites corporal suffering
Immortal are those even though mortal

9. One Time Offer

Life an offer given by Almighty once
Surely second time there's no chance
Value it use it in proper time and place
Mind it the offer we can never replace.
One time offer but limited time cover
Forget not first come first endeavour
Delay is quite dangerous to recover
Sad is his lot who undermines however.
Wait not waste not avail the opportunity
Let's do our assignments with committed loyalty
Followed by punctuality, sincerity, devoted honesty
Without forgetting our honesty and integrity
Our duty makes our life meaningful
Let's make the priceless offer purposeful.
One time offer never comes again
Hug it love it enjoy it without disdain.

10. Woman

Beauty is woman, woman is beauty
Without her presence desert is society
Mystery of creation centre of attraction spell bound
Power of construction and destruction as well all around
Daring, caring, and sharing personality
Having dashing, lashing, embracing quality
No similes, metaphors suffice to glorify her beauty
She is unparalleled incomparable icon of simplicity.
Woman, woman thy name is beauty
Indescribable beauty of humanity
Hope, confidence, trust in reality
Loyal, royal, incredible purity.
Woman, woman thy name is sweet home
Thy presence makes home a heaven
Heart of home, life of offsprings
Soul of family, whole of all things.
Inspiration, aspiration and motivation
Stimulus, stimuli and core stimulation
Thou are nourisher, nurturer, and caterer
Ultimate shelter holder next to Creator.

11. The World is for Us

Beautiful gift to the mankind
Multipurpose lies in it's behind
Some to revive some survive
Detached but heartily He likes
Luxury and adversity side by side
Incessant motion of day and night
Sun constant moon revolves aside
Myriads of stars with azure sky.
Seven colours in eye-catching rainbow
Six sisters seasons one after other
Born on the Earth equally show
Pity and joy for no higher nor lower.
The world with natural scenic beauty
Serene, tranquil, solitary nobility
Impels lovers to indulge in creativity
To search for peace eternal divinity.
The world full of barren and fertile land
Up and down, smooth and rough road
Flowers with fragrance still some thorns
All these are horns to people pretty warn
Each moment here highly valuable
Each particle of creation purposeful
Your wrongs are right for someone
Someone's rights are wrong for you.
The way you take this world bad or good

Similar is the way it undoubtedly moulds
If you love the world go not astray
The world will never and never betray.
Be sanguine the world is for us
Be positive the world is with us.

12. Walls

Built with purpose
Walls around us
God can dispose
What we propose
Limit your limits
Unlimited summit
Never aspire fire
Unwanted desires
Stop to explore
World of valour
Squeeze the scope
Much awaited hope
Foolish to ignore
The safety walls proffer
That keep us inside
No foes enter outside.

13. Rose-Eros

Eros the explicit meaning of rose
Rose an implicit meaning for Eros
Eros lies in rose sensuously symbolising love and softness
A connective between lover and beloved passionately brings closeness
Rose intensively writes rhythmic songs of joy and peace
Between two unseen unknown souls stands as a bridge
Life without eros like life without heart bitter and naked
And heart without feelings is heart without lungs, beat
Rose is a rose the consent to surrender self
A promise to accompany forever not to escape.
An eyewitness to the occurrence in life to second
The presence stimulates and makes the duo understand
Let's be a rose to spread fragrance of Eros
Forgetting the place from where we belong thus
Let's be a device of simile or metaphor for poets
To be a meaningful meaning for poetic assets

14. Escape

Escape from regular study
Makes students all rowdy
World of mind turns to desert
From mankind humanity departs
Escape from daily duty
Escape from responsibility
Invites own acute poverty
Ruins of maturity, vitality.
Escape from ideal society
Not only spoils life's beauty
But also loses one's virginity
Dragging towards futility.
Escape from a cage of bondage
Removes all ravages of salvage
Gives voice to raise privilege
Moment to pay homage to praise.
Escape from relatives inside
Absolutely imperative outside
Pushes to be negative aside
Positivity suppressive behind
Escape from joint family
Life cheerless obviously
Escape from humanity,anarchy rules in reality

15. Thankfulness

A source of achieving peace in mind
Imprinted inside heart ever remind
The moment of helping in adversity
How meaningful His gift of humanity.
A massive weapon to win others
Humble regards we surely gather
A centre of attraction to be reason
To make one smile being a mission.
A ripple of pleasure to wash away
All mental ailments in every way
Leaving behind some impression
Unforgetfull that compassion.
A large heartedness to share
Inner voices of life so aspire
Take and give no second thought
To balance is not to anyone hurt.
Tools of good manners to culture
Future generations to nurture
Assurance to build bright future
Society remembers it's maker.
To convey thanks no personal loss
Benefits not meagre in cosmos
Blessings shower from all corners get ready to garner.
A source of achieving peace in mind
Imprinted inside heart ever remind

The moment of helping in adversity
How meaningful His gift of humanity.
A massive weapon to win others
Humble regards we surely gather
A centre of attraction to be reason
To make one smile being a mission.
A ripple of pleasure to wash away
All mental ailments in every way
Leaving behind some impression
Unforgetfull that compassion.
A large heartedness to share
Inner voices of life so aspire
Take and give no second thought
To balance is not to anyone hurt.
Tools of good manners to culture
Future generations to nurture
Assurance to build bright future
Society remembers it's maker.
To convey thanks no personal loss
Benefits not meagre in cosmos
Blessings shower from all corners get ready to garner.

16. Life is a Great Lesson

Life teaches how to become a survivor.
Life is calculation of addition, subtraction, division, multiplication
In arithmetic, plus minus in Algebra and measurement in mensuration
Life passes through ups and downs
Sometimes smooth somewhere rough
Stony, thorny, winding, snaky, slippery
Anyway life stimulates how to run like a river
Life witnesses falling, rising and rising, falling
Stumbling, crumbling, crawling, struggling
Smiling, moaning, shouting, howling
Still life proposes how to stand still embracing, greeting
Like unmovable mountain, everything
Life meets several birth and death, ruins and creations
Defeat and victory, flood and drought, promotion and degradation
Mishaps, adversity, uses and abuses, love and betrayal
However life never abandons, hopes, attempts and trials.
Life never counts days, nights, months and years
Always duty-bound committed dedicated for years
Time bound, routine bound planner, searcher and explorer
Life Geographically surrounded by plains, hills, water, forest as well as habitation
Life not the whole, perfect and complete but a means of collaboration.
Life has a meaning, purpose , beauty and dignity
Life is an agent makes us live, feel, smell touch, see and hear glory of humanity

Life sweet or bitter a great lesson for mankind
Leaves something miraculous on the sands of time.
Life is a great lesson learn from it, read it deeply, follow it wholeheartedly
Very success will bow down your feet undoubtedly.

17. Reflection of Love

Limpid like water
Each one's desire
Reflects better
Can any not admire.
Life savior
Tastelessly tastier
All of us roister
Like bees cluster
Around flowers flutter.
Life's lighter
Huelessly brighter
Rainbow discolor
Before the loveliest
Love of lovers' labour.
Painter of colour
Powerlessly mightier.
Undefeated soldier
Confident winner
Never give in failure.
Hope ensure.

18. Suicide

How do you that you have full rights upon your life
Your life is not yours, someone's gift
Amalgam of mother's love and father's joy
A divine contribution to mankind
Think not that you have rights upon your life
To decide whatever you like
Suicide not a game to play with pleasure
Not a solution or to take steps major
Suicide not a leading path to pursue forever
Pushing own near and dear to dungeon of danger
Suicide not an intended option or act of kindness or goodness culture
Demonstration of cowardice roles staged
Human life the result of long ages of meditation
Abundantly enriched with the feelings and emotions
Beautifully made with senses and imaginations
A computer like brain and intellect to assert what to do and what not
Enough courage to face every challenges of any range or sort
Human being the mostly liked and foremost creature of creation
Gifted with all sublime traits of His own
Sweet voice to sing melodiously
Creative power to recreate things gorgeously
And many more indescribable
Why then o' human you take to suicide ?
When life is so cheerful and colourful
You are born with a purpose inevitable

19. Worth of Words

My inner strength to speak the whole world
Makes me bold enough to win one's heart
Like flash light of show magic and music
Intensively entertain the mass enthusiastic
Being the owner of words be high ecstatic
As words simple having a characteristic
Some easy some complex some phatic
Bitter or sweet, emotive or sarcastic.
The soul of my life immortalised forever
Emotions of heart whisper to swing
Chariot of my mind fly without wings
Blow like the wind touching all things
Flow like a river downwards to mingle
So many meanings of a word single
Use it to make one smile and delight
Gauge words in insight and foresight.
Weapon to subdue all opposite forces
Spirit to motivate means to embrace
A bond to friends talisman to allure foes
Coming from core of heart words like rose
Tender and fragrant love to propose
Pass words for passing a message
Get rid of bondage to take a mileage
For emotions of expression carriage.
Mighty power to change whatever may be the range

Devils can not revenge ability to face any challenge
Let's be the words of knowledge and courage
Be our mind of versatile words a world storage

20. Autumn

Days become shorter to enhance the life span of nights
Silvery moon plays hide and seek with great delight
Be a season like autumn to extend helps with might
Never refrain aloof from duties already assigned.
Falling of the year approaches with falling of leaves
O‘ deciduous trees why so disheartened and sad in grief.
Pain tests your patience to take away all strife
Let's wait and watch something happens right.
Migration of birds drive to the matting world in thy advent
Most cheerful moment of life arrives at the place to mat
O' autumn of fruitfulness how often you for them sets a set
To fulfill the golden dreams of life with a assured target.
As there is no fall there no rise the nature's law
How can we harvest much we desire without any sow
Emptiness in life guarantees the fulfilment of every gap
O autumn profound grateful are we when you alights on nature's lap.
Thou are really the poetic erotic inspiration
For poets derive a lot from you for vivid expression
O' human beings let not worry about your autumn of life
Only autumn prepares a stage to invite our spring of life.
The Autumn adds to the beauty of nature
How pretty seems the portraiture!
All seasons have some specialty and peculiarities
Here, Autumn shows a new way to start
For old to depart and new ones to impart.

21. Some Moments in Silence

Some moments in silence
sitting on the sea beach
my ears can listen to His whispers
Some moments in silence
beneath the cerulean sky in verdant field
my eyes can behold His unseen power.
Some moments in silence
passing through the deep forest
my mind sparkles in the darkness
Some moments in silence
when the sun sets in the west
my heart dances in calmness.
Some moments in silence
closing your eyes strive to see
the world within you
You will come to know
who you are and where you are
to play your roles and how.
Silence makes many a miracles
Miracles ensure the pinnacles

22. The Age Of Innocence

The golden age in the annals of humans stage
Ever remembered as engraved in golden letters
On the stone of manhood like holistic heritage
Sparks in azure of family as the crescent moon glitters.
New chapter opens in the conjugal life of couple
Heavenly pleasure showers upon all members
The more you peruse, the more it seems simple
Books of humanity stored in the self of life's chambers
Devoid of understanding the age of innocence
Unware of things and people around afraid not of anything
Hollow of feelings of senses the age of ignorance
The apple's eye in the group to sensuously allures everything
As fragrant as blooming flowers to pervade fragrance
As limpid as water having illusiveless appearance
As transparent as mirror to reflect the reality in vehemence
Scarless moon in the social ember the age of innocence
A new beginning in human life comes with nothingness
Leaves the mundane world with quite nakedness
Unlike the other creation, twice would they appear with sameness
Rare of the rarest to think and introspect the fullness
The golden age in the annals of humans stage
Ever remembered as engraved in golden letters
On the stone of manhood like holistic heritage
Sparks in azure of family as the crescent moon glitters.
New chapter opens in the conjugal life of couple

Heavenly pleasure showers upon all members
The more you peruse, the more it seems simple
Books of humanity stored in the self of life's chambers
Devoid of understanding the age of innocence
Unware of things and people around afraid not of anything
Hollow of feelings of senses the age of ignorance
The apple's eye in the group to sensuously allures everything
As fragrant as blooming flowers to pervade fragrance
As limpid as water having illusiveless appearance
As transparent as mirror to reflect the reality in vehemence
Scarless moon in the social ember the age of innocence
A new beginning in human life comes with nothingness
Leaves the mundane world with quite nakedness
Unlike the other creation, twice would they appear with sameness
Rare of the rarest to think and introspect the fullness

23. Prayer without Ceasing

A bridge to the Almighty
Wireless connectivity
Reaches the sensitivity
Echoing realm of serenity
Ripples of ceaseless prayer
Opens the eyes of silence
Compels Him to see the flare
Of confidence in penitence
Prayer a powerful tool for change
The heart of rigidity and abhorrence
Beholds the light, slavery inside cage
Birds of love comes with a message
Prayers in the hands of a sage
Become a weapon for salvage
Saves the world from the savage
People we must pay homage

24. Family File

Family all in one organization to share
Everything of life that is absolutely fair
A bond tied with rope of love with care
To break, no outsider or any power dare.
School is the institution for qualification
But family is the school of humanization
Where character is framed with perfection
Good manners imparted with correction.
Land of compassion and conviction
Kindness, forgiveness and affection
Where mistakes are rectified with patience
To be human like human with confidence.
Encircled with unity, possibility with identity
Place of safety and security of ideality
Undefeated forces of equity, integrity
The haven of peace and tranquility.
Where mother teaches how to manage
Father the instance of how to encourage
Brother justifies how to fulfill responsibility
A sister to show how to serve hospitality..
Grand parents the store of wisdom to endue
A son dares to dream how to subdue
Family built on foundation of love
Stands on the pillars of faith and hope.

25. Where is Love?

Like water cachaside the core of heart
The more you open, the more it comes out
No end, even ceaselessly one can distribute
Let be not so greedy to heartily contribute
Like mountain drinks heavy rainfall
In no way bows down head at all
Gusty wind of filth can never shake or turn
Nor scorching sun of anger or heat can burn
No tornado of hatred or envy can devastate
Always ready to face any challenge at best
Like air freely moves touching everything
No indiscrimination, no bar for crossing
As generous as Nature for nurturing
As awesome as flowers for rapturing
As magnetic as magnet for capturing
What a magical force for hypnotizing
Love is like deep, dense and dark forest
Each naughty mind and heart can arrest
Love is where life is, life is where love is
Taking all carbon oxide, fresh oxygen begets
In the terrestrial life, love is a haven to rest
Love never gets pluck in every kind of test
Where love is, if you search in you
You will get the answer quick and due

26. Sunset

Sun neither rises nor sets always remains constant
Gesture and posture changed while in distant
Rising sun of mankind steers the wheel of nation
Whereas the setting sun guides all to reach the destination
Gold like the setting sun, glows never fades
Priceless the values, nowhere never degrades
Setting sun never sets in the west
After a long drive of journey they just take rest
To prepare a routine and chalk out a new plan ahead
Leisure with coolness of mind gets refreshed
Messages in shape of twilight worldwide pervades
Heads to head the posterity to save the mass from outside raids
Passing through the various states of life time
Can understand the situation to quickly decide
What to do what not, what is wrong and what right
Sunset the stage leaving moment to invite the newness
To fill the gaps lying vacant due to dearth of freshness
As the time is moving on the way of rapid globalisation
Something we have to compromise for sophisticated Innovation

27. Beauty of Nature

Lovely creation of the Almighty
A priceless gift to humanity
Mesmerising her scenic beauty
Embellished with tranquility
Dancing waves in murmuring river
Reduces high temperature of fever
Humming bees fluttering round flower
Electrifies the lust of mating lovers.
Creepers to skyscraper trees in forest
Leaves to flowers and flowers to fruits
Enhances the travellers' deep quest
Tempted to density compels to rest
Waterfall allures visitor's senses
Hill and mountain far stretches
The mind and heart of viewers catches
Stimulating some to ink rhyming muses.
Take care of nature to nurture with peace
Be faithful and loyal to grace with bliss

28. Two in One

Parents and children like two in one in kind
Unconditional love they have, must remind
Incomparable under the sun nobody can rescind
For ages the connection never be defined.
Blindly believe each other without any suspect
Complementary to one another in all respect
Unique bond of relation -pure, stern and divine
Union of two in one together
As long as the world exists a diamond forever
Covered in the pot of affection no one can uncover.
How natural and divine a matter to discover
For children how genuinely parents are rovers.
An embankment erected over pillars of confidence
No time and tide can demolish their credence
A combination of milk and water to balance
How can we segregate one another to blemish

29. A New Dawn

Where there's ending there's beginning
Where there's is beginning, there's ending
Life is amalgam of days and nights
Do your duties to claim your rights
Every day comes with a new dawn
Greet with heart, let not take it a fun
Never ponder over days already gone
Something you have, let it be done.
Every day comes to an end to leave the stage of performance
For the forthcoming episodes to open the entrance
No one is perfect to fulfil the needs of life
Every moment of life imparts knowledge worldwide
Everything is valuable, may be more or less
Everybody can, at least, be capable of filling the dash
Feeling to think something wrong or right without face
Otherwise an uphill task to win the sublunary race

30. Attraction of Beauty

ANudity of a woman not actually beauty
Rather allures the lust of a man
Love lost there where and when arrived reality
Naked painting spoils something in pain.
Beauty always plain and simple more humble
Simplicity and humility mother of real beauty
Diamond like attraction divine perfection
Sparkling like falling stars glaze the purity
Painting of a lady throwing a rose
Like doctors giving patients a painless dose
Much attract heart and mind with deep force
Seeds of love sprouts in the eyes of beholders
Attraction of beauty comes from inside
Beauty is not beauty that looks outside
Unless it touches the core of a thing
Beauty is nothing but an intense feeling
Truly said, things are not what they seem outside
As the bait baffles the fish under the water to it's side
A horse without rein how can you ride
We must take a little time to do before we decide

31. Golden Moments

Life itself a golden moment never comes again and again
Has brought me an opportunity to initiate literary campaign.
The golden moment of childhood swayed in the swing of love and affection
My all round fluttered a bee like mother to feed me with pamper and compassion
Moment of adolescence blooms like colourful flowers
Enriched with the fragrance of pretty dribbling showers
Centre of attraction in the eyes of much awaiting beholders
Never be escaped from the greed of recognised lovers
Adulthood a moment of dreaming the world of possibilities
Impossibility hides it's face under the veil of creativity
Catching the moon in hand to captivate her silvery beam
Searching the best that lies in the world of whim
Old age the return of the day of childhood
Helpless, dependable for a little care of manhood
Each man to pass through this golden moments
Sometimes make terrible, sometimes enwrapping in merriments

32. Glory of Indian Culture

A practice of respect to elders caressing the feet
Bowing down head being so humble when we meet
Love to youngers with a warm and open heart kiss
Showers upon them divine blessings eternal bliss.
Togetherness during diverse festivals and ceremony
Unites one and all with the knot of peace and harmony
Free to read write and speak any language one can wish
To express feelings and emotions exquisitely not to miss.
No restrictions to accept any religion to worship
Without hurting the others their sentiments and fellowship.
Staunch beliefs to coordialy regard women as goddesses
A massive teaching to others wholeheartedly to possess.
Culture of my country a source of knowledge
Undoubtedly one may eagerly take this privilege.
Varieties in attire,food habits and customs in all
Enormously allure the myriads of heart and soul.
Indescribable, uncomparable is Indian culture and heritage
However past and remote nobody can captivate in cage.
All over the world are prevalent my culture
With the hymns of humanity mankind to nurture.

33. Twenty Twenty One

Whole year of twenty twenty so panic
Under the brutal reign of the pandemic
Shaking the worldwide beauty scenic
Many a flowers faded before blooming
More terribly shocking than other natural calamity
On the part of mankind unbearable that's fatality
With the advent of twenty twenty one in anxiety
Shrieked the spread of contagion with no intensity
Let the twenty twenty one be enormously enriched
With strength and powerfully nourished
Unleashing the era of love and peace
Pervading the world with divine bliss
Let the year be highly glamorous and fabulous
Every creature be happy and prosperous
The pen in the realms of literature conspicuously focus
Be flourished, progressive and gloriously conscious
Let the year come with a new dawn of hope and confidence
Sowing the the seeds of love, harmony and patience
To harvest the fruits of eternal joy and happiness
Humanity be established over the world in abundance.

34. Pen and Paper

Pen and paper two in one like bread and butter
Elements of fulfillment complementary to each other.
Inseparable and lifelong friends in all weather
Universal architect to design and reshape the future
Power of a writer to present their inner voice
Mightier than sword, bolder than soldiers to impress
Upon powerful enemies of slackness to suppress
A weapon to sloganise to wake up the oppressed
Means of communication for the untold stories
Narrator of the narration to applaud the awesome glories
Paint the picture in words person to person in diversities
Creating one world of humanity, love and peace sans varieties.
Like little drops of water makes the vast ocean
Like the skyscrapers built by the human mason
Small piece of pen and paper makes eternal creation.
Imperishable monument for generations to generations
Pen ploughs the land of barren white paper
To harvest the fruits of innumerable literature
To safeguard the art, humanity and culture
To feed the mind with positivity, hope and faith to nurture.
Paper bears the whole world of mastermind and imagination
To offer the mankind universal message for humanization
To filter the hearts of fools and follies with sermons
To enlighten the world of ignorance
Pen and paper nothing but haven of stars and moon

In absence of sun they can shine world with divine boon
A shelter of writers, thinkers, changers and reformers
Accommodates all to expose them as better performers
O, pen and paper for the sake of mankind, my dear
May you live long; stay blessed and evergreen to cheer.

35. Imperishable Wealth of Mankind

We can travel the whole world without moving our feet
Second world of the creation always ready to greet
The mankind anytime anywhere any moment fit
For all generations to come never try to quit.
As long as the first world of His Excellency exists.
Books are the imperishable wealth of mankind
No thieves can steal the part or whole behind
No sun no rains no wind no winter of any kind
Can dare to touch the body, heart or mind
No such mighty power or strength can ever divide.
Unlike the human friends never think to betray
Good companies are books allow not to prey
Long live dear books let's join in the mission to pray
Let's be a part and parcel of who rarely entice to go astray
Stand for us in every situation without any delay.
More than a mother who feeds the mind with positivity
More than energy that empowers to face adversity
More than a teacher who teaches how to live in society
Like unseen spirit foretells how to tackle calamity
Make one feel good, think better, do the best activity.
All master minds of world class gather together
To make a master piece rare of the rarest in any weather
Like the birds of the same feather flock together
Whose makers dedicate their entire life for others

If we have such things in hands nothing to bother
Food for the hungry water for the thirsty available everywhere
Tonic for the patient, stethoscope for doctors required anywhere
Light for darkness, shelter for homeless problems nowhere
Breath for life to survive long elsewhere
More suitable more portable more applicable here and there.
Storehouse of knowledge, idol of courage
River of enthusiasm, ocean of rapture storage
Oasis in the desert to remove the mirage
For transportation of expressions a better carriage
Establishing peace and humanity a well constructed barrage.
Books are like garden with diverse hues of flowers
Books are like homes to provide comfort and ease to shower
Aesthetic beauty and all-round safety the need of the hour
All in one to serve mankind the fulfillment of human desires
A voice raised reward for the good and punishment for the bad
A challenger, changer to build a noble shade
A promise to make many a thinkers, writers, poets and dreamers
A commitment to mould a man into a moral being, a reformer

36. Dawn of a New Day

Every dawn comes every moment everyday
With conspicuous life changing merriment
Dawn of a day emerges with various gifts
For diverse people or things slowly or swiftly to tender
To lay the foundation of posterity sought for future
Nuptials changes the couple with refinement
In words, deeds, thoughts, nature and conduct betterment
In opinions, views, action, reaction and settlement
When two unknown souls coalesced together for achievement
A new creation to hearty greetings with benign consent.
Motherhood juggles a woman with solidarity of eternal divinity
She stands still like mountainous patience with integrity
Ocean of unconditional love unfathomable and pity.
Turns to the goddess of peace and tranquility.
A reason for the honour of beauty, truth, a creator with dexterity
Right decision on time for right person at right place makes destiny
Topples down all doubts, complexity in fair scrutiny
Sweetness of life showers like honey
Enlightening the arena of heart however tiny
Enables to keep the balance of peace and harmony
Dawn of failure turns up with the sunrise of success
Like the say no fire without smoke in the boiling furnace
Transition in life is a must to cordially embrace
That drives towards the goal of destination face to face
Everything takes time so not to be harassed.

37. Whispers of Memories

Time changes, days followed by nights
Colour fades away from the beautiful sights
Stage by stage mind runs to heightened foresight
Memories whisper as light peeps through skylight.
Memories memorable like inspiring stories
Nowhere lost, never dies, works like calories
Silhouette never stays far away from its pole
On the surface of water cannot make a hole
Changes the sanctum from one to other just the soul
Likewise, leg far behind memories whole.
Memories like creepers coil if get an asylum
Cannot escape unless you captivate in your life album.
Unforgetfull are memories however bitter or sweet
Warns us beforehand any danger when we meet
Betray not it's master, may not be a cheat
Memories are reality sometimes hurt or hit
But likely to enrich the mind, the fest and feast.
Life without memories there's no twist
Some memories retained, some takes time to melt like mist
Memories are as lively as life itself
To impart something good without any self
Takes pain to rectify mistakes for life's sake
Unseen are past memories nobody can hijack.
Flutter like bees, glitter like stars round the moon
Appears like morn, noon, afternoon and evening boon

A friend in need at times a memory lane
A farsighted guide to lead with no complain
An expert to be believed staunchly no problem
Warm up the doleful heart like a flame.
Like farfetched imagery multiply glory and beauty
Present preserved in past and past paves the way for posterity
Truth can never be wrapped in a blanket of lies
The more you hide the more it flies

38. Let Me Whelve

Let me whelve in the ocean of love
Will stay there like pearl beneath water
Sucking the water of compassion
Flood the earth with the soil of humanity
Let me whelve in the core of your heart
Will whisper the story of magnanimity
Kissing the cheeks of mankind
Bloom the flowery smiles on their lips.
Let me whelve under the soil to out
Each moment everyday will sprout
To spread the aroma of integrity
For the reshaping the society with novelty
Let me whelve in the clouds of adversity
In the blink of eye will rise like the dazzling sun
To remove the mirk of helplessness
To wash away the tears of failure forlorn
Let me whelve in your eyes as divine tears
Will blow out to lessen all your sorrows
Already housed inside you since you know
The complexity of life, assure you, nothing worry to bear.

39. Family is a Home

Family a home where dwells every stage of human to frame
Elders, older and youngers together in a frame
A workshop of manhood where moulded each -hood
Childhood, boyhood, youth and old ones to brood
Family loves each member to grow and glow
All members the pillars of family to owe
A shrine of divinity, a place of equal responsibility
A paradise of budding flowers to offer identity
Love to live in family, family will never betray
In no circumstances, she lets you go astray
Shouldering responsibility makes you confident to sway
In the swing of happiness leaving not far away.
Family an embankment of affection to hug near and far
Strength of commitment and fulfillment by far
Ideality or ambience, chastity or integrity nobody can mar
Living in a family seeks no permission, nor any bar
Lucky is the family to watch diverse roles of her children
For whom prepared a stage of action, mono action to train
More fortunate are those born and nurtured time and again
Staying far away from family makes one looser, nothing to gain
Family devoid of hypocrisy, conspiracy and pretention
Free from monopoly, slavery and corruption
Free from impositions of fee for training or taking prevention
First school of human beings to provide moral education
We all are the pillars of Family, family the pillars of society

Mother the backbone, father the head in reality
Love is foundation, understanding the strength and unity
For plan and structure, heartfelt thanks to the Almighty.
Where there's family, there's no scarcity in anything
Family is life, family is breath, family is everything

40. Music

Like first love, fia touch fast reminds first
Music is water that quenches inevitable thirst
Music is food that assuages lingering appetite
Leave not the chance to crest the outreach height
Music is scientific experiment to find peace
Sad his lot who far away from this divine bliss
Listen to the sweet voices and watch the magic of music
Undoubtedly will fabulously stimulate to be erotic
Life is a music player, play it with devotion
Will free you from unhealthy suffocation.
Music is a key to the happiness, calmness and silence
Opens the gate of mellifluous melody of credence
Music is the sun that enlightens the realm of obscurity
With the golden light of purity, solidarity and divinity.

41. Sweetness of Words

Sweet words touch the core of hearts
With sweet sounds make ears sweet
Enliven each life of its kind
Forgetting deadness of enmity behind.
A balm for the ailments of mighty anger
Heart exults to accept without being avenger
Time, place and persons surrender
Each complexity of understanding under
Sweet words can act like a magic stick
Opens the knot of life's fabric
Mesmerizing millions in the land seraphic
Haughty naughty attitude calmed down
With the aroma of charm hypnotic.
Change a change making a being moral
Capacity to mend a broken heart natural
Turning world of every informal to formal
A diamond forever everywhere, every time can sparkle
My words, my inner strength can promise to guide
A renaissance to reverberate reflection inside
A commitment to reshape the dying culture outside
In every walk of life the chariot of equity can ride.

42. Let me Promise

Let me promise not to show superiority
Guest s of two days, pride and vanity
Not to be proud of youth and beauty
For everything perished leaving the scar of entity
Let me promise to rectify all mistakes committed
Mistakes are the pillars of success to be achieved
Life without mistakes is life half completed
Mistakes are like potion to be enriched.
Let me promise not to think bad of others
As every action has reaction together
Bad things, O bad things no one can forget
No one can even remember good things in life's set
Let me promise not to admire the the wrong
Not to be hesitant to praise the right
Supporters to the injustice more fatal than contagion
More injustice not to encourage the right person
Let me promise to remain aloof from rape and murder
Not to alter human to animal to cross the border
As what I am is a beautiful gift of my Lord
And what will do in life be a gift to God

43. The place we Live in

A society made by humans to live in
A place to accommodate living beings
Not just sets of castes, creeds
A shade of gregariousness to breed.
A shelter of love and affection to share
Promises each other to take care
A land to sow the seeds of togetherness
Dream to harvest the crops of goodness
A laboratory to experiment equality and unity
Towards the solidarity for humanity
A haven of creators with manifold creativity
To exposé inner talent of universality.
A storehouse of language, literature and culture
Houseful of habits, customs, tradition filled with rapture
A confluence of artist, singers, painters vested with texture
Amalgam of smiles and tears, birth and death in mixture
Teaches the hymns of "unity in diversity"
*Together we stand, divided we fall"
There's one religion called humanity
Life in mundane world not devoid of rise and fall.
An earthly abode of God who loves the image of human
He himself incarnated in this loving form
To establish peace, harmony, and fraternity with devotion
To save the mankind from the demon of dissension

44. Nothing Born Immortal

When there's rise, there's fall
Death is sure to be followed by birth
Empty vessel be filled with water
Sorrows and suffering emerges out of mirth
Each day witnesses some growth and development
Along with innumerable loss and achievement
Blessed are those beneficial to mankind
Stand for the side of righteousness behind
Cursed are those having no purpose to feed
No one remains to remember the bad to bid
Nor some are left to forget the good to heed
Each one to leave this world of existence in stead
Immortal are good thoughts, good deeds
Enriched with vitamins of positivity
Love, peace, harmony to sustain humanity
Some memories are as fresh as air for life to divinity.

45. True Friendship

Friendship is to understand each other
Strength in loneliness, stamina to stand together
Cooperation between two persons or races
No matter in pleasure or sorrows faces
Dedication and sacrifice in words and action
No place of selfishness and pretention
A bridge between the two sides of poles
How can body be separated from soul ?
True friendship stands on the foundation of love and compromise
The rapport acts as blessings in disguise
Amalgam of adjustment and toleration
In mind and heart an alluring attraction
Faith, loyalty and confidence pillars of true friendship
A lifelong solution to each kind of hardship

46. Sound Of Silence

Keep silence, you can hear everything clear
Each corner of the world vividly seen, dear
You can discern the existence of Creator
Even in the closed eyes of silence better
The ripples of silence float to the Almighty
Wakes Him up the echoes of silence in tranquility's
A perfect and awesome tool to hide your anger inside
If you earnestly employ in every walk of life
Can vanquish all enemies of negativity
Suppress the mighty forces of animality
Pervading the fragrance of nobility
Silence magnificently captures mind of humanity.
Keep silence, you can talk to the mankind
For ages of meditation can do nothing to remind
The volume of silence echoes worldwide
Reciting the hymns of life, feeling pride
Not a matter of jokes to culture in a day or night
The heart of silence can behold the deep and dark side.
Silence the language of gods and goddesses
A means, a lot of things inevitable to express
Spontaneous is the narration, nobody can suppress
Prolific are the artists owing to easy access.
Sublime, thy name is silence
Can devoutly create a suitable ambience

47. Men of modesty

Men of modesty real heroes who can subdue
The enemy of anger, envy forced for peace to sue
Men of modesty are the epitome of humanity
Angels of promises to keep and embodiment of serenity
Men of modesty are men of self-effacement
Show not there any achievement
Neither in words nor in action of perfection
Like fragrance of flowers spread in all directions
Men of modesty are men of reticence
Adopt the divine weapon of silence
To tackle all situations with full confidence
They believe in themselves to win others' credence.
Meekness their best technique to solve the problems
Compel the persons in front of them
As hypnotized to surrender instead to blame.
Men of modesty are men of humility
Thoughts and experiences adds their magnanimity
The way they culture shapes their identity
The way they behave teaches the society.
Lifelong self-conscious are men of modesty
Far from undue awareness of own identity
Modesty, not age or growth, shows one's maturity
Humanitarian attitude in life begets modesty

48. Who a Poet is

A dreamer of the dreamers dreaming golden future
Rules, regulations, manners, etiquettes and law maker
Not for a group, class, or race but for mankind universal by nature
Truly said,. "Poet is an unacknowledged legislator'
A thinker from the depth
Well-wisher of the mass
Role model, icon of the social beings
Lover of beasts, insects every creatures living or non- living
An avid reader of nature, behavior and character
Searching goodness in badness and often badness in goodness
A prolific critic, vivid admirer, and lucid appreciator
Analyzing, explaining and scrutinizing uniqueness.
An inventor to invent new ideas, concept and knowledge
Worldwide relevance in every section of life age after age
A discoverer to unfold the unknown under any foliage
A path finder to the savages for eternal salvage
A fluent speaker of diverse topics on life in society
A narrator of the untold stories penned by the Almighty.
A versatile writer of emotions, feelings and experience
No arena of life untouched, unseen in his or her prudence.
A moulder, mender to mend the disorder of bemoaning heart
A mason to build the skyscraper of hope and ambition
A goldsmith to make pretty ornaments of words
A barber to cut the growing hair and nail of corruption
A performer of Wordsworth's solitary reaper, or leech gatherer

Sometimes seen as a beholder, painter, joker and ring master together
Sometimes a beggar, shopkeeper, little by little to gather
Pearl from the heart of conch, solace out of anger
A reshaper of the broken world of mankind
A universal teacher and preacher leaves something behind.

49. What is Poetry

Poetry is as lively as life to enliven as caricature
Sings the songs of pain and pleasure in mixture
Laughs by heart to make others laugh in critical juncture
Mourns over the sad demise of humanity and culture.
Poetry is as conscious as divine spirit
Ensures punishment for the habitual culprit
And honour to those who rescues life from social pit
Beyond the ambit of intellectual summit
Poetry is the recreation of the existing world of Almighty
Something in a new shape in quest of veracity
Something in a way emulating his master in dexterity
A bridge between the creation and creator in serenity
Poetry is an art of painting the words in the hues of emotion
A rainbow in the azure sky of clouded depression
Panacea to all unsocial evils of humanization
A transport to carry the goods of inner expression.
Poetry is the treasure trove of unending beauty
Unfazed, undying, imperishable assets of society
Mind refreshing tonic to energise nerves with sanity
Reservoir of love, peace, harmony and unity
Poetry is the lucid and vivid expression of heart
Unspoken myriad stories in flowery words
When lips are slack, pen makes possible to word
To shape the destiny of man transforming into a bard
Poetry is the fertile land seeded with crops of knowledge

Readers are the consumers to have this privilege
Lucky are those happens to take the mileage
Harvested throughout the year, unlimited storage
A lesson to teach the whole mankind
Amidst the struggle how to survive.

50. Understand The Poor

No education needed to know the poor
Never underestimate them as moor
A heart is enough to
Read poverty
No techniques sought to eradicate paucity
No promises, no speeches fill the need
A little empathy required to take heed.
Be a support to withstand the load
Expect not in return even to hold
Be a balm in their physical pain
Openheartedness make them dare to gain
Be an umbrella in the sun of the poor
Let them forget the past, ensure
Self respect they have never want to spoil
Truly are they the sons of the soil
Can go on without food, but never deceive
Place or position of the poor, we have to perceive
They can die but never betray
In no circumstances, can go astray.
Understand the poor, poverty be elevated
Be motivator, let them feel not isolated.
Poverty not a curse, a blessing in disguise
All those who have been rich, once poor in riches
Selection of right track towards the destination
Can help us to overcome poverty without hesitation.

51. Spices of Betrayal

Blind belief over anyone may cause something wrong
Without judging persons with voluntary help let anything come
At anytime, any moment, anywhere with a gang
Overconfidence over near and dear
The fruits of fatal consequence one has to bear
All sources of cheers dive into the ocean of tears
Excessive freedom to anyone as humans
The reasons of much endurance in all unhealthy situations.
Unless and until taken quick introspection
Too much of greed makes one kill own humanity
Makes him forget to choose the things of reality
However, the greedy can never enjoy their property
Bad or good unable to comprehend
Being captivated his or her head under heinous trend
The betrayers succeed but defeated in the end.
Long absence in distance greets betrayal of legacy
Offers an opportunity to create a field of conspiracy
Chalking out a plan takes more time for accuracy.
Water-milk closeness may disclose the weakness
As only the deep rapport can make easy access.
Free and frank hearts often twined in whirlpool of losses
Slavery of cherished hopes and unfulfilled desires
Pushes to the fantasy of life and conspires
To reach the goal of selfishness even it leads to pyre

52. Magic of Language

A divine gift of God to the whole mankind
Humans are most special for this heights of insight
Empowered with the enriching instinct
From all others humans are perfectly distinct
To use the mother tongue the language of heart
Never leg behind to acquire other languages fast
A bridge between the two races dwelling in separation
To communicate each others' feelings and emotions
Thankful to those for the perennial invention
Contributed wholeheartedly to the civilization.
There's magic, music and melody in language
Ever felt in speaking, listening and reading with mileage
Recorded in the written text the story of the rise and fall
In various genre of literature in all to speak all
Offering the society a limpid mirror
To see the countenance of past in future.
A language the best means of expression as we wish
Tells us the diverse art, culture, tradition and customs of ages
Language, sitting in the corner of house in leisure
Helps reading great minds of world with pleasure
Can show the scenic beauty of inexplicable nature
Presents before us the most remote part of universe
Drives to the realm where no stones remain untouched
Moves around the globe to explore the cosmos.

53. Language of Silence

Silent expression of heart not absent
Language of silence everywhere present
Heart touching and mind blowing its language
As sweet as pious nectar to rid bondage
A benediction forbidding mourning, lamenting
A prayer for knocking the door of peace enchanting
A doorway to the heaven of dreams to visualize
Utterance of hymns of salvation to realize
Language of Silence ripples in the ocean of mind
To kiss the shore of forsaken loneliness to shine
Echoes worldwide and reach the core in no time
Unforgetfull its sound, rhythm and rhyme
Language of Silence is the mother of all languages
Since time immemorial has been attracted the sages
Means of communication in the hands of hermits for ages
To connect with the Almighty directly for messages
Language of Silence non symbolic, unwritten but fluently expressed
Blessed are those who happen to embrace
Silver lightening in the thunder of others to grace
Golden future of generations to come in progress.

54. Dancer, Dancing and Dance

Dancer not simply an artist or entertainer
Who can steal the heart of taut audience
A performer on the glorious stage of confluence
Who bets on life for the cause of influence
The melodious song, the rhythm of music and prance
Dance not just tripping, twirling but artistic and aesthetic beauty
That mesmerizes zillions of mind to lay aside their anxiety
Life even dances with the dance of a hoofer
Mind dances with the dazzling dancing posture of danseuse
Heart dances with the whirling steps of ballet dancer.
Dance is in us, feel it, hug it and love it to give us energy
Knowingly or unknowingly we practice in smiling
In walking, speaking, listening, speaking and even sleeping
Life without dance is full of lethargy
Like a log of dried wood in piling
Dancing is one in all and all in one to say passion, profession or recreation
Nonverbal, musical, shimmering and colourful life's expression.

55. I am Poem, Not a Poet

I am a poem bloomed in the garden of literature
Emerged in diverse colours in various forms in texture
Sometimes poetic, sometimes prosaic in manner
Whatever may be, I am a poem to be a alluring genre
Like the wind I never leave anything untouched
No matter rich or poor, sweet or bitter
Like the river I take away with me all others dreams
No matter small or big, high or low in rank or cadre
I am the easiest method of transporting and transforming
The load of untold emotions and feelings
Somewhere to turn someone's tears to smiles
In the wings of imagination can fly to beyond miles
Somewhere to make others cry in the overload of desires
I can pass the universal truth and knowledge to mankind
Uninterrupted, untried from ages to ages over time

56. Mother

Simple but a pivot character of woman
The best and super among others
Blessed with divine love ,purity and eternal sanctity
Undying character of the creation of Almighty
Continuous running fountain of unconditional love
Washes the filth of her children
She does not know how to take back in return
Deep love makes her more stable than a mountain
More tolerant and liberal than the Earth
To bear the load of aching pain.
Embodiment of the angel of kindness
Can digest every dose of anger and hatred
To pour upon the showers of affection
As if golden moments of opportunities to destination
Above all pretension and hallucination
She keeps on sharing what has been gifted on donation
Even life without second thought of introspection.
Goddess of forgiveness for her offspring's
Forgives their all mistakes or misdeeds smiling
Stands as an encouraging force of healing
Mends the broken heart of helplessness inspiring
Resets the disorder of haughtiness by heartily caring
Immortal soul, undefeated fighter, dreams gatherer
Unparallel moulder and reshapers
Unquestionable personality forever

57. True Love Never Dies

Behold not the colour, age, caste or creed
Search not the millionaire or crorepati to feed
True love is love to love above and over all to heed
That's the only needs of hour we ought to need.
Seek not any season, day or night to embrace
No particular time, person or place to grace
Desire not of belonging to the same religion or race
Love is love to love that exists always natural and fresh
Arrange not any gorgeous function to celebrate
Dream not to put on any ornamental habiliments immaculate
Invite not many a people to accumulate
Money, or power to subjugate
Love is love to love above all never ever calculate
True love like stars shines in dark
Like gold glows in fire
Like diamond sparkles beneath the sea
Like pieces of clouds float in the sky
True love is pure love never dies
Blows like wind to share
Flows like river to dare
Nurtures like nature to care.

58. Ebb and Flow Of Life

Like a river or sea life faces ebb and flow
Like morning sun it glows and fading sun slow
Not always stable, things to swallow
Time the mighty power often makes high and low.
Rise and fall the twin flames of life to aspire
More rising, more falling law of nature to inspire
More falling, more rising certainly never conspire.
Think not what you see is smooth and plain
Unless putting the steps nothing to obtain
Humans are not always humans to be humane
Humans the mixture of both beast and human.
Life the amalgam of light and dark
Without the presence of dark light never spark
Light and dark combine makes life grow
If there's no present, there's no tomorrow.
Sorrows and smiles stand together to make a life strong
Right cannot be right unless there's a wrong
As two pieces of ropes make the swing to sway
Both sides of life enable ones to move away

59. Lady of Versatility

O, mother, thou are the lady of versatility
How can I describe your divine personality.?
Let me pardon as I dare to express my stupidity
Extraordinary and protean character of immortality.
O mother, the lady of divinity
Embodiment of love, peace and prosperity
Epitome of affection, compassion agility
Goddess of kindness, forgiveness and magnanimity.
O mother the lady of justice
Can never shelter any injustice
Your the morals, you are the ethics
Easily all the tasks how you can accomplish
For the children you are the life and soul, an ultimate bliss.
O mother, the lady of beauty and serenity
Like the ocean in vastness or stability
Like the flowers to emit fragrance and tranquility
Like nature's caring, healing and hospitality.
O mother, the lady of immortality,unfaded your colour of maternity
Unparalleled your vision and mission in profundity
Incomparable your unconditional love and service in sanctity
Days, months, and years insufficient to narrate thy identity.
O mother the lady of making my character and destiny
My nourished, enrapture, care taker, and hive of honey
You are my teacher, mentor, friend, philosopher and guide
It is for you, by you and because of you I am here to enjoy the ride.

60. Secrets of Justice

Lady, eyes enwrapped with black cloth band in tranquility
Can never see near and dear or outsider in Identity
Before her to join hand in hand in any activity
Unseen is better than seen to discern reality
Justice thy name is impartiality
Divine trait of humanity
A balance in left hand in quiet stability
Gives away rights to one and all in certainty
Measure with great poise whatever quantity
Equal things for equal price in quality
Justice thy name is equality
A slogan for world fraternity
A sword in right hand replete with assurance
To vanquish the culprit in credence
Might is right remained in essence
In each poetry as conceit hidden in vehemence
Justice thy name is the Almighty
Dedicated to harmony and solidarity

61. Living Goddess

Simply a woman transformed to a living goddess
How unable are we to see her angelic face
Blessings in disguise for those who can embrace
A living goddess of love and compassion
Unconditional and spontaneous reverberation
Unspeakable her emotions
A living goddess of kindness and generosity
In her caress all ugliness turns to beauty
Dressed in the priceless apparel of simplicity
A living goddess of forgiveness
Who can only pardon the children's guiltiness
Can understand the untold feelings, ignore the weakness
A living goddess of commitment
Never fails to achieve fulfillment
Enriched with requirements
A living goddess of sacrifice and dedication
Remains above and over all illusive intention
Free, frank, pure in thoughts and action
Mother can be compared to everything
But not everything to mother or her feelings

62. Panacea for The Time

TIME is passing through a crucial moment of panic
Let each one promisingly bear with situation without being a cynic
That will be the panacea for the time to whole mankind
Who are directly or indirectly responsible, we must keep in mind
Social distancing from one another vociferous ointment
Free of cost but needs strident willingness a natural treatment
Apply this formula with a passionate commitment
To save you and all others from the pervasive predicament.
Masking the face the blessings in disguise to prevent the epidemic
Make it a habit, a part and parcel of life being enthusiastic
Washing and sanitizing hands and face with antibiotic soap or sanitizer
Be and make others be an ardent motivator and mobilizer.
Staying home and sharing the family in actions the panacea
Definitely with hundred percent will remove your inertia
Having been enriched with such effective tonic
Why reticent, come forward to expel this without letting it be chronic.

63. Prayer Of The Day

O Lord God the emperor of the living world
See, how your creation is in peril
Mankind thy first and foremost creatures about to derail
The youth the future maker of nation
The preserver of your creation
Retire from life without remuneration
Much before their superannuation
Working classes far away from livelihood
Pet animals deprived of food, their broods
Silence reigns over solitude
Warriors against Corona unable to brood
Over the pandemic situation so rude
Remain not in deep silence
Time is fleeting far distance
To take your test no patience
Your eminent sons and daughters
Your worshippers, appreciators
Singers, men of letters, sculptors
Artists, architects, orators in all
Leaving this mundane world with your call
Deserted are we children as orphans quite helpless
To stand on our own legs to shoulder the stress of loneliness
O saviour, emerge in a new form
Stay unseen but kill the germ
Save the world, save generations

Selfish are we human beings
Still are we all your offsprings

64. Time Can Change Everything

Time can change with phase by phase
Since time immemorial to ages
Day to night, night to day no one curtails
Dark to light, light to dark no entails
Wrong to right, right to wrong
Un/conscious are we the throng
Why then fight for the height
For the rights for the might
Forget not that we are parasite
We can, in our own will, never expedite
Time can change color, age, beauty
Green to yellow, yellow to grey
White to black, black to white
Child to boy, boy to adolescent
Birth to death, death to birth
Time can change the stages
Poor to rich, rich to poor
Smiles to tears, tears to smiles
Higher to lower, lower to higher
Why then emulous to excel desires
Time can change state, feelings
Love to odium, hatred to love
Anger to peace, peace to tantrum
Water to snow, snow to water

Stone to sand, sand to soil
Hillock to plane, plane to hillock
Stream to river, river to sea, ocean
Even desert to tilth, tillage to desert
We have to wait and watch the best
Inevitable are the change better to accept
Time can change attitude, belief
Reality to dreams, dreams to reality
Negative to positive, positive to negative
Oasis to mirage, mirage to oasis
A home to heaven, heaven to hell
Time can change you
But you cannot time
Time can change hue
But hues cannot time
Time can change everything with no stop
No matter, whether rough, tough or soft.

65. Happy Mother's Day

One day is not enough to say
Happy mother's Day today
Wish each day a happy day
For mothers to freely enjoy
Respect her feelings and emotions
Sentiments, thoughts and actions
Suppress not what she to express
Listen to her words not to disgrace
Share her what you have in mind
Care her each habits to delight
Neglect not her wishes to excite
Ignore not her problems to light
Happy mother's day in practice
Let's offer her bliss and justice.
On this auspicious mother's Day
For her peace and joy let's pray.

66. Speaking Shadow

Depression not my silence
Nor any weakness
Nor retirement from life's business
My strength my loneliness
Shows me light to see the truth
Obviously the ultimate fearlessness.
No deception, no pretension
In my loneliness of extension
No reluctance, nor any distance
Just to bridge the generation gaps
May be platform to avoid the mishaps
May be the world to reshape
Commitment to do the wonders
Know not how you ponder
But I am sure to surrender
Me to the mighty mender
To forgive this offender
And beg His apology to render
Something extraordinary
Something miraculous
To unlock the doors of secrecy
With assurance and accuracy.
My loneliness my secrets
No isolations no regrets
Loneliness makes my fate

Keeps me away from hate
All my disorders are reset

67. Atonement

Human life absolutely messy not by chance but by nature
No human perfect to tidy all filthy and askew texture
Of bad and good, haps and mishaps, life is a mixture
Atonement helps to repair or replace the fracture
Gives a chance to bring back the former posture
To commit mistake is human
No mistakes, no rectification to gain if refrain
Perfection comes only when regularly drain to train
Gone are the days when blindly believed things plain
When something lost is something to regain
Causing injury or doing wrong deeds quite common
Unless and until some atonement summon
Intact are the things lie in human
Nothing happens to change in their domain
Foolish are those who leg behind to attain
A bridge to join the ugly past and lovely present
A tool for bettering and battering things to look decent
Surrender oneself to accept the reality not indecent
Heart broadened, mind brightened in atonement.
That drives all humans towards final achievement

68. Positive Thoughts

Men of positive thoughts strongly believe themselves
That's their fortitude to help self delve
Let them explore the world of failure
With the spirit of vigour and valour
Men of positive thoughts rarely leg behind
Emulous attitude enraptures their mind
Sort out all problems in any situation with cunningness
Sanguine of the best of things around weakness
Positive thoughts confidently rights the wrong
With the hymns of optimistic ideas not being hung
The swing of ecstasy touches the summit of triumphs
Everything seems bright and colourful nymphs
Think positive, do positive, responds positive
To make yourself constructive adjectives
To beautify, dignify and simplify all initiatives
The end will be magnificent perspectives.

69. Confinement

Budding flowers never bloom inside pristine jar of confinement
Broken hearts never sing the songs of enjoyment
Wingless birds never dare to soar high up in the firmament
Caged birds never dream of the sweetness of amusement
Frogs inside the well never think of the beauty of nature's merriment
Bookbased knowledge never helps in mind's nourishment
Daylight never opens the eyes tied with a clothe band
Sumptuous food turns sour to the mouth closed over command
Water tastes bitter however sweet and cool in brand
Haven with locked doors and windows a dungeon to the end.
Men of confinement nothing but blind and mute
Dumb and lame forever inside wall to wall to commute
One thing to the society must they contribute
Bondage and slavery a voice of the time to compute
Never lasts long on the holy earth even without dispute.
Time can change the scene and sight to contribute.

70. Rhythm of Nature

Listen to the rhythm
In the cooling breeze of winter
In the gentle caressing wind of spring
In the intense scorching sun of summer
In the river's bubbling and murmur
Never let us go astray in fear.
Listen to the rhythm
In the twittering of birds melodious
In the buzzing of bees lustrous
In the whirling of tornado fabulous
In the loneliness of darkness gorgeous.
Croon and dance bounces heart so joyous.
Listen to the rhythm
In the lullaby of a mother
In the dense gusty rushing of weather
In the weaving dance of flowers
In the sudden gushing of showers
Replete with ecstasy in every hour.
Every moment a moment of rapture
In the hypnotic rhythm of nature.

71. Fear of Failure

Dread not the fear of failure
Like a barking dog it does allure
Hug failure and see its valour
Can change your fate, be sure
Thou are owner, failure a fiendish thief
Who just wants to maraud your belief
Still twitchy to encounter the holder
Who withstands to confront the marauder.
Fear of failure never be clouded for keeps
Let you renew your bash and leave
To heave a euphoric sigh of relief
For a golden opportunity to receive.
Within the core of failure lies the treasure of success
Pushes to the ocean of bid to seek pearl of solace
Regress not harking the roar of the fear of flop
Throw the trap of try and toil to the beast fright to engulf.

72. Knowledge and Wisdom

Knowledge is acquisition of thoughts and ideas
Germinated in various faculty of broad areas
Wisdom the practical knowledge that stored in theory
Applied in real life giving lots of experience
Man of knowledge and man of wisdom
Differently exist in the same kingdom
Both are the pride of a nation
Help steering the benevolent administration.
Man of knowledge a teacher in the four walled room
But man of wisdom a preacher, a changer in cosmic doom
Knowledge is an art but wisdom a science
Without practice no gulf gauged between commonsense and conscience.

73. My Masters

Born helpless was I with nothingness
My mother my master made me sit, stand, walk and speak
But for her mastery myself be utterly paralyses
Jeopardizing to the dungeon of dumbness and lameness.
My teacher my master made me listen, read and write
To understand, rectify, realize the purpose of life
To grab and retain to make use of future insight
Enlightened my path of journey to crest the destination
Society, friends, relatives and situation taught me how to survive
Birds, animals, nature together nourished my mind to revive
Books travelled me to the unknown and brought my notice to imbibe
The essence of life preached how to live and let others reside.
What I am now is only for all my masters contributions
Who have moulded me, guided me with dedication
Unrepayable the debt of my masters in my life
Except my humble gratitude for their service, endless try.

74. Promise

One action better than thousand promises made
Promises are few words uttered be pretermitted
Actions the accomplishments of assignments
Make the doers heuristic with the right complements
Promises are hollow men's weapons to subdue the situation
Promises are future nobody can ascertain its application
But actions present most worthy of comprehension
Instead of being uncertain in words better to live on actions.
Promises are dreams before sleep in the bed of snow
Sometimes promises delude the promiser nobody can know
Thus, break of promises may shatter the blood relations
Like bookish knowledge useless unless appertain to he or she owns .
However, promises given be effectuated at any cost
To prove oneself vigorous cognizing power of words
Let the words be glorified as stars shine in the dark
Both the giver and the taker be the legacy of a mark.

75. Morning Comes

Morning comes daily no reason to worry
Everything takes times, no need to hurry
Morning comes with a divine gift
Fixed for everybody, no one can shift
However, may it be a challenge
Let's encounter together we can change
Morning comes with something for me
That may not be for you to see as an epitome
All are not equally born with the silver spoon
Don't be afraid of that, morning will come soon
Morning comes with a bouquet of flowers
To invite some to the bed of roses a sweet hour
But for some with a series of trials and tribulations
To test the potentiality and to strengthen ambition.

76. A Wish to Live

Have a wish to live for others
Without any bother
March forward further
Promise to stand together
Have a wish to live
For seeing dreams
To make them true
Nights be shaded hues
Have a wish to live
Life is a lesson to teach
Each moment enriched
Something to preach
Have a wish to live
Not to take but to give
Things to perceive
Not to deceive
Have a wish to live
Changes are needed
To sustain peace
Let's embrace divine bliss

77. Solace

Humans are we to face lots of challenge
Every day the clock of fate moves incessant
Passing through the changes of time
Summer and rain, spring and winter
Life be sure to saddened with load of depression.
Pain is where life is comfortable
And life is where pain is inevitable
Support of someone relax in distress
Extending helping hands expresses solace
Man gets dissatisfied, disheartened out of failure
When what he or she needs is consolation
Whether in words or deeds it does not matter
Some moments standing for them can revitalize
Resets, regains the lost hope, rebuilds life
Togetherness in time of demise of relations
Sharing experiences during pleasant functions
Giving shelter to the homeless, the helpless with compassion
Caring the poor, feeding the slum dwellers with affection
Guides the people out of track and reshapes humans in right direction.

78. Bloom Like Lily

Let's bloom like a lily in the pond of society
Even germinated from the sludge of vices
Dread not for all ensuing causality
Till thou are inside the limpid water of spices.
Forget not neither water nor mire can touch the lily
Promised fairly to serve the purpose daily
Sterile and unsullied her glossy body
All godliness, goodness and holiness she can embody
Becomes the ladder to the unseen power
For her Lord staying far away smiles to flower
Waiting with lifelong sacrifice to surrender
To heal the ailments of mankind in the prayer something to render
Let's stay inside the circle made by water of sanctity
Can blemish you no filth of humanity.

79. Some Mortals Are Immortal

Death is inevitable sparing nobody under the sun
No mighty power nor any technology can prevent throng
No discrimination in caste creed colour
High- low, rich-poor and superior-inferior.
Everybody once born destined to die one day
Law of Nature to balance nobody can betray
One has, accordingly, some roles to play
After the bell of life rung, leaving is must, no more display.
But good deeds with love and dedication
Make the mortals immortal for generations
The footprints left behind reminds the mankind
To be inspired and motivated following the great mind
Men of immortal are those who sacrificed life for the cause of goodness
Sow the seeds of love, peace, harmony with large heartedness
In spite of being mortal imperishable the contribution
Stored in the reservoir of humanity unending the distribution.
Some are great by birth, some are by actions
Men of greatness shine like stars in the heaven
Showing light to the travelers on their journey of expedition
Unconditional workers are the men of immortal

80. Men of Serendipity

Men of serendipity are persons exploring the horizon of newness
Present the mankind a priceless gift the doorways to uniqueness
Over years of sweat and toll, unrest and turmoil in return in loneliness
Unseen the near and dear for years far away from the closeness
Men of serendipity are those who wander in quest of unknown
Make them beggars in luxury, the scholar gipsy of erudition
Inquisitiveness takes them to the antique places, things forlorn
Bridging the gap between fantasy and facts, passion and vocation.
Men of serendipity by nature creative, artistic, constructive and positive
Experimenter, explorer, extinguisher, enthusiastic path finder of initiative
Lost in the world of ingenuity emerge like sudden downpour or falling stars
From the limitless amber of inventiveness to the earth of alternative
Serendipity makes a common man uncommon
Natural, a moment of happenstances not on and on
Does the miracles however, infrequent in nature
Unlike other source of knowledge one can never culture.

81. Be Positive

Blame not yourself being victimized
Let's take time to surmise
See things positive to humanize
Yourself with others to rise
Up to the mark you ever realize
Better to love who hate you
Detest them who love you
With the passage of time
Everyone comes to your line.
Never think of I, me and mine.
Do what you love to do
Love what you want to do
Changes will come to see
If you change your self in glee
Negativity sure to away flee.
Blame not what you are
Blame why you loose there
Ignore not what need of the hour
In garden does not bloom flower
Unless you plant with care.
Ask to yourself who you are to expect
What, how, why and where to suspect
You are the questions and answers
You are the problems and solutions so far
Behold how shine at night all the stars

Be not selfish to accept what you expect
Be not betrayer for what you couldn't prospect
Be not looser for your negative attitude
You have logic, reason and aptitude
Be positive to obtain things lying in rectitude

82. We Are One

Black or white, rich or poor no matter
Brahmin or Kshatriya, Sudra or Vaisya no matter
What matters is we are all offsprings of one creator
Human our identity irrespective of caste, creed and race
Humanity our religion obey it follow it and embrace
Nothing be achieved as rival to other community
Can do nothing in conflict, heinous brutality
Grace of the Almighty abandoned to destruction
How can think of better construction?
Be not the man enemy of man however sovereign
Lucky are we super duper being a human
Born are we with a meaningful purpose
Forget not the second chance never comes
You are the chance, you are the opportunity
Let it be beneficial for the others in any calamity
Surmise your own place and position
Where you stand, walk, run full of emancipation
You are the war, peace, and bliss loaded with divinity
You are the violence, nonviolence equal in positivity and negativity
See options are many before you to select
The way you follow will offer you the same, yours is the rest.

83. Rejection

Rejection without reason
Means of cloudy illusion
A furnace to consume
Nothing remains to resume
Rejection with right decision
Suppression of nihilism
Refines the malpractice
Forever to abolish
Let rejection be purposeful
To make situation meaningful
Mind not ever any rejection
Rejection entices inspiration
Inspiration entwined in stimulation
Opens the door of culmination
Many a causes' call invitation
Rejection of love and affection
Leading frustration, botheration
Ultimately builds a mansion
Of hope, faith on foundation

84. Biscuits

Destiny of the poor lies in it
Favorite bread and butter to choose
Contentment and encouragement to survive
Saviour of several simple lives
Fire of anger extinguished, snow of poverty melted
With a packet of chef biscuits
Full satisfaction reserved for kids
All in all as sumptuous food to feed
Low in price, small in size but purpose so high
Available everywhere to get it right
Appetite loses its sense and sure to die
Filling the belly of emptiness to fly
Many a men crest the destination nothing to lie
Common things common life always simply favours
Sufficient simplicity fruits of hard labours
As the hungry men never long for sweet flavours
Owners of littleness, self satisfaction harbours
Men living on biscuits can face every situation
Impart how to adjust and compromise with reverberation
Who can better understand what and how life emulates
Let the mankind follow the mechanics and techniques to inculcate.

85. Beauty of Nature

Myriads hues paint the nature unfaded
Eyes felt mesmerized Bewildered her creator and fainted
Beyond imagination but realized
How unfathomable the beauty of nature
Beholders hearts throb up in rapture
Azure sky with limitless clarity
Milky way's spotted within
Embedded in image of sanctity
Tranwilizes the broken hearts erasing sterility
Verdant forest in tranquility makes a veil
Grassy land being a lofty sari to wear
Mother earth gets matured to wed
Her life partner passing time in flowery bed
What a communion I really indebted
Earth decorates herself in golden light of the sun in day
All hers offsprings and associates feeling gay
In the beauty of nature she does lay
Sheltering the millions of lives on her lap
How startling things reshaped the way.
Night changes her habiliments
With the silvery moonlit garments
How colourful and bright each moment
Sparkling the sights with diverse pigments

86. Calm Clouds

Clouds soar when roar
Clouds spark when dark
Rain cats and dogs
Gusty wind warmly hugs
Dark clouds vapour moulds
CALM clouds clear doubts
Allures mind to be kind
What a wonderful scene behind
Blue sky seen high
When calm clouds tie
The knot of serenity
Nature looks glorify
Azure sky happily croons
When calm clouds roam
Wind plays the piano gently
Verdant Earth beholds eagerly
Confluence of blue and white
Soothing heart's delight
East and West intermingle
When calm clouds invite

87. Giving Thanks

Small things great action no fees in return
No time required easily can be spoken
Littleness but heart of greatness with impression
Makes a man noble, humble in collaboration
No wealth gets ruined, no pride lost
One day with passage of time we to mix with dust
Character and personality lives without any cost
In everybody's heart as the scar till the last
Giving thanks leads to deep relation
Pain of ego and envy lessened with effectuation
Reshaping the destiny of falsehood in right direction
Interaction in reality two way communications
Thankfulness makes a man magnanimous
If the receivers and givers are unanimous
Places a position demonstrating a class
In giving and taking there will be no clash

88. Luminescence

Friends come and go, some help, some escape
A true friend shines in a friend's mishaps
A beau remains with a lover till his richness
A real wife sparkles in husband's helplessness
All teachers feed the learners knowledge more or less
A right teacher illumines in student's slackness
Humans are selfish by nature changing place, person and action
But a man standing for others luminescent of creation
Men of luminescence are men of godliness
Still scintillating in the corner of mankind in stillness
Men of luminescence are men of reformation
Born to save the lovely and lively world from extinction
Men of luminescence are men of letters
In the realm of literature forever glitter

89. Psalm of The Earth

Nature's gift to mankind
Almighty's grace so kind
Earth only place for life
We live till she is alive
Forbearance her strength
Kindness her identity
Mother of wealth
Everything offers her entity
No earth no existence
Feel and fill her presence
With love and assurance
Care and share all your opulence
Let her live to live
Leave her to glee
Let your strife flee
Stop making her cry

90. Homeless

NO home but peacefully roam
Here and there for a sojourn
Leaving for others alone
Nothing stable but everything viable
The whole world their home suitable
No worries nothing to carry
Having nothing still found merry
No dreams to emulate
No desires of wealth to accumulate
No anger, no envy to revenge
Everyone deserves their homage
Small is their deeds but take heed not to hurt
Small their ambitions with open heart
Void of possession but full of compassion
Loaded with nothingness tied with deep relaxation
Homeless but not, no, never cheerless
No arms, no enemy to defend still fearless

91. Shades of Love

Like magnet love attracts
Like electric current it distracts
As inevitable as death nothing to be sure
As to place, person, situation limpid water gets impure
Love without self and expectations turn to worship
Perpetually made a novel relationship
Obsession builds a haven in one's mind in love's grip
Unhurt, untried the travelers on the way of the trip
Blind to see the near what to speak of distances
When deliberately fails to comprehend ensuing circumstances
A position of unconditional reverence waving in intensity
Opens the gate of the castle surrounded with undefeated possibility.
Life without love and love without love unused utensils
No place in the cosmos can anywhere conceal.

92. Child

A abode of the Almighty
Filled with sanctity
Innocence and serenity
Ignorance and Verity
Embodiment of purity
Divine verginity
Base of humanity
Pillars of love, peace and tranquility
A land needs tilling
A blank paper seeks inking
An empty pot needs filling
A source of joy and cheering
A piece of gold to be moulded
The way you want to be made
Neglect not to go ahead
Time to be lekker utilized

93. Aubade

Aubade pens for sweet dawn
A song never forlorn
Dawn croons by heart
Laments to depart.
Let us greet with love
For making day bloom
Discarding gloom
Spreading fragrance soon
Ready to get up the sun
From the bed of horizon
The east opens the door to come on
To enlighten the world with light on
O dawn thou are song
When morning bell rung
Day utters in tongue
Thy name in sacred song.

94. Humans without Humanity

More than wild beasts having no rationality
Who, by themselves, ruins their own identity
Who molests own mother or sister, thus blind
Leave nothing in the society so unkind
Humans without humanity unsocial element
No complement, no supplement in achievement
Help adding social, moral predicament
Losing five senses, responsibility and integrity in poor nourishment
Humans without humanity detrimental by nature
Take away all pleasure and rapture
Leaving the ambience a hell to
Nurture
Now is the time humanity to culture
Humans without humanity lifeless beings
Devoid of five senses, dearth in dealings
An empty piece of pot having nothing appealing
Humanity an weapon to adopt for humanizing.

95. Aura of Autumn

Aura of autumn allures the passersby in glee
Mind captivated in the trap of beauty can never flee
Paddy leaves dances in the ripples of wind
How can they defy Nature's order to rescind?
Fragrance of fruitfulness pervades all over the sites
What a lovely sight autumn's gift to delight
Season of harvest brings enthusiasm in tiller's family
Stored are the blank treasuries with abundant riches gently
Mildness of winter kisses the green leaves and grassy land
Cleaning the grey dusty filth from the greenness bowers
Sets a stage of poets and writers to assemble
For sharing views, ideas opinions of sagacity to avoid trouble

96. Duty A Great Teacher

Duty not just action to accomplish
Not just promises to fulfill
Or responsibility to shoulder
The best teacher guiding me forever
Duty shows me the mistakes already committed
Accordingly guides me from wrong deeds prohibited
In duty comes ups and downs, failure or success
Teaches me to follow the right process
Warns me, advises me, moulds me in various places
Makes me known all about my weaknesses
Makes me understand the worth of things
Looked down upon by others on dealings
Duty my light, my courage and knowledge
Frees me from the clutches of savage
My anchor, my holder, my moulder
Makes me immortal even my death to ponder

97. Telling Lies

Habits one cannot abandon
However unpleasant created situation
Harbinger of temporary pleasure
Like oasis in the desert
Building castles in the air to measure
Lifeless empty heart.
Heart overloaded with lies day by day
Self punished in the swing to sway
Becomes the mark of unread message
Deleted often from the memory phase by phase
No space or time avoids remembering
Printed their names in red letter in the calendar
History records the history of liars in the pages of time
Literature specifies the specialties to chime.

98. The World Within

Closely look at what within you
Intermingling seven hues
Making life colourful
Foolish to be mournful
A mixture of land, sky and water
How eager to mix each other
Inspire of unfathomable remoteness
Are they collide one another
For their own selfishness?
Fire to burn unwanted abandoned particles
Let it costume to explore untold articles
To offer a great taste of chronicles
With a novelty of shrewdness
Fruitful is the creation of the Almighty
When diversities fall in love of unity

99. Wisdom

The way you talk to others heaps a pile
The language you speak that makes one smile
The words that enters one's heart and cheers
Washes away from the face priceless tears
Sharing all to others for pleasure
Brings undoubtedly divine rapture
Change oneself to change something to culture
Becoming a rainbow in someone's clouds
An eraser to swipe away everybody's wounds
Picking up thorns from the way
Be the swing to sway
All are the real wisdom one can culture
From one's life who is a great teacher.
The way one sleeps to dream the future
Experience of success and failure
Enriches one's present to nurture
The unseen and uncertain future

100. Power of Words

Bitter are the words uttered in high volume
Hazardous to heart's tender gloom
More vigorous than the sword to tease the temper
Tears the heart apart nothing can hamper.
Sweet are the words muttered in slow and soft voice
Can conquer every force of enmity
Matter a lot to rejoice when they embrace
Love and affectionate words unites the diversity
Words are poisonous and full of embrotia as well
The way one uses makes the difference that can swell
As water falling in drain destined to be impure
Same water intermingling in pond or river limpid and pure
Bitter words so painful can leave undeleted scars
Till death gravely dwells inside the haven of heart
Reminds the unbearable pain remain unexpressed
Never dare to collaborate the souls much oppressed

101. Even when I Fail

Even when I fail I never lose hope till the end
For failure undoubtedly enables to stand and encourage like a friend.
Life having two sides positive and negative
Can never exist without being cooperative.
Life is not what you think or I
As your wrong may be right for me.
And your right be wrong for others
Life is beautiful strive not to make it defile
Patience and perseverance needed to survive.
Even when I fail I never worry or hurry
For failure enlightens the path to glory
It is failure that brings plenty of chances
Fills our mind with tons of confidence
Failure not really failure unless we confess.

102. Fear

Fear born with wrong deeds
To warn you how to succeed
Fear grown with negligence
To realize penitence
Fear develops with doubts
Make one shout loud
Fear is close to us
Ruin when conspicuous
Fear is in us
We are his boss
Sometimes better to have fear
For authorities to administer
For subordinates to obey order
Fear often saves us from evil doers
Drives towards righteousness if we endear.

103. The Way You Smile

The way you smile different from other
Makes me smile nothing I bother
The way you smile as natural as rainfall
Makes me cheerful nothing remains fearful
The way you smile more magical than magic
Pure entertaining what a mesmerizing tonic
The way you smile replete with melodious music
Heart exults mind raptures quite hypnotic.
The way you smile makes me forget everything
Your smile food of my life caring and nourishing
The way you smile germinates in my heart the seeds of love and peace
Nothing more I require stay smile and smile be the evergreen bliss
O Smile thy name is divinity
Reason to live better and happy humanity.

104. Smile

No money to pay for your smile
Think a little deep for a while.
SMILE is natural unending flows
More you smile more it glows.
SMILE a mirror of body tells the truth
Force of unwillingness never can hide inside tooth
SMILE like fragrance touches each mind
Heart exulted sorrows leave far behind.
SMILE a shower of rains from heaven
Heavy thirst quenched relieve pain
SMILE a charm of life to embrace
A renaissance reverberated impress
SMILE a balm for mental agony to lessen
Life becomes energetic dynamic to regain
SMILE a magic of life real and mesmerising
A melodious music wholeheartedly appealing.

105. A Change to Change

Flow like rivers downward
Stop not on the way like coward
Mingle with others to widen
Realm of mind, something to pen
Blow like wind with no hatred
Touch the heart of bad and good
Difference you have made
Not the people or goods.
Be like a flower to bloom
Coming out of deep gloom
Be free and frank in deeds
Without having any greed
Be a change to bring a change
In your hands lies the range
Let changes be a pledge
Everything will glaze

106. Talented, Poor And Hopeful

The poor are talented they can adjust
Compromise the life as they are robust
They know how to suffer and derive pleasure
The depth of weakness they can measure.
The talented are indifferent to the normal
Abnormally makes them different and formal
They hide themselves in the search of newness
Dedication, and sacrifice without devotion meaningless
Both the talented and the poor hopeful of their duties
Considering the service as the blessings of deities
The poor are poor in wealth but not in sharing mind's money
And the talented poor in luxury but rich in love, peace and harmony

107. Experience

Experience makes a man practical to explore
The sweetness of joy one can taste
However, experience comes with flying colours out of failure
Success never hides in any corner of the world in rest
Experience the mother of wisdom
Enlarges the sphere of kingdom
Already tested gets pluck seldom
Man with experience be confident
Every challenge face independent
Being sufficient enough, prudent
Experience assures the fruits of endeavour
Ceaselessly if we garner to culture
Victory in life granted in our favour
Mankind, experience can nurture.

108. Nature Is For Us - 1

Nature is for us, we are for nature
There's is life where there's nature
Where there's nature there's rapture
See, what a mesmerizing texture !
Unlike other planets the Earth is unique
Worldwide wrapped with beauty scenic
For the wounded soul efficacious tonic
Lively toys of joy for children with no panic
Miraculous is nature's creation on earth
So lucky is she bearing on her lap
Innumerable things, Imperishable wealth
Stored for mankind to enjoy with mirth
Beautiful because nature is colourful
Peaceful by nature, graciously merciful
Growing, glowing, sparkling and truthful
For every creature meaningful, purposeful.
O humans, embrace the priceless gift
Of the Almighty, we have to greet
With warm love and peace without greed
For nature is mother everything can breed.
Nature never betrays, if you love by heart
Has universal knowledge to impart
Always for us, with us in pain and pleasure
Being a nourisher and well wisher forever

109. Nature Is For Us-2

Nature is for us to nurture
Her how can we torture?
Amalgam of living and non living
Plants, animals and human beings.
Nature is for us to guide
Open is she never can hide
More beautiful her outside
More meaningful her inside.
Nature is for us to feed
Always takes our heed
Seek her help in need
What she cannot breed
Nature is for us to teach
Mankind of loving outreach
Helping hands never to cease
Nature is for us to enrich
Nature is for us to shelter
No one can reshape better
Than the nature of Nature
From her something culture.

110. Humility

Two friends moving on the way to destination
Found a bag unknown
Undecided with confusion
Let's see one said
The other so sad
Not to open the bag
Thought to throw as rag.
No way found at last
Sat under a tree first
Finally agreed to open
Amazed to see inside then.
Seven bundles of notes
Nearly seven in lakh
Made them totally upset
May be or may not be fake.
Long run discussion took
About to chain the hook
Aadhar card saw inside
With mobile number on it.
Greed never touched them
Conscience allowed not to defame
Called on phone to return
Being learnt recalled the lesson
As knowledge begets humility
Avarice spoils integrity

111. One Is Enough

Have not many a friends one is enough
As the moon among the stars is tough
A friend who shares pain and pleasure
Undoubtedly the priceless treasure
Like the lamp post and mile stone of life's path
Days and nights over years stands undisturbed
A guide a driver can drive the car of friendship unpaid
Still no expectations in any adversity can withstand.
The one among all dares to second a bossom friend
The vigour and valor like soldiers in all situations to defend
Losing such a friend in life a great defeat to meet
Remember forever not to force him to fall your feet.
One is enough who is caring and fair
Committed dedicated devoted and bare.

112. Mother's Love

LOVE above and over all love is a mother's love
Unconditional her love eternally so tough a hub
Common is mother uncommon her love
Parallel to woman but unparallel is love
Unfathomable depth is her love endears
Unending wealth is her love enriches
Ambrosia is her love nourishes every moods
Panacea is her love nurses the wounds
Blanket of blessings is her love saves from sun and rain
Powerful balm is her love soothes all pain
All divine spirit lies in her love empowers the child
All heavenly peace is her love pacifies life
A strong boundary is her love encircles with safety
An enchanted castle is her love with security.

113. Thankfulnes

A source of achieving peace in mind
Imprinted inside heart ever remind
The moment of helping in adversity
How meaningful His gift of humanity.
A massive weapon to win others
Humble regards we surely gather
A centre of attraction to be reason
To make one smile being a mission.
A ripple of pleasure to wash away
All mental ailments in every way
Leaving behind some impression
Unforgetfull that compassion.
A large heartedness to share
Inner voices of life so aspire
Take and give no second thought
To balance is not to anyone hurt.
Tools of good manners to culture
Future generations to nurture
Assurance to build bright future
Society remembers its maker.
To convey thanks no personal loss
Benefits not meagre in cosmos
Blessings shower from all corners
Of the world get ready to garner.

114. The Mirth of Love

Love is life that teaches how to survive in fullness
Love is light that enlightens the heart of darkness
Love is power that conquers the land of despair
Love is a law that deals all sorts of affair
Love is a magnate that attracts and bind each one
Love is nectar that immortalizes the deceased one
Love is a stream of joy that delights the quiet
Love is a shower of rain that quenches thirst quite
Love is mesmerizing magic that the audience enlivens
Love is melodious and mind-blowing music that the deaf can hearken.
Love is divine bond that no one can break whole
Love is indestructible bridge that connects two souls
Love is hope that illumines the path of future
Love is belief that unlocks the door of compromise forever
Love is understanding finds the solution to each problem
Love is talisman for driving away all social evils like flame
Love is adjustment love is cooperation
Love is accommodation love is toleration
Love cares and shares without expectations
None other than love can rescue the world from destruction.
Life without love a heaven or hell
Think my dear where you are to dwell.

115. Expectations

Expectations the root of sorrows and anxiety unavoidable
Snatches away pleasure peace happiness unbearable
Expectations of parents push them to pit of repentance
Demolishes the citadels of dreams in front of their presence
Expectations of children roll them to the well of persistence
Building castles in the air without having ability or competence
Much expectations of wife turn the husband to a scrounger
Changes nature behaves like a.stranger inviting own danger
Much expectations of human beings greet the advent of depressions
That consumes up the spirit of humanity with exploitations
Better not to have much expectations in life
A blessing of Almighty regard and use it to avoid strife
Everybody be forced to go astray
Eventually nothing keeps one away.
Remember all things shall pass away
Let life live and pass in a simple way.

116. Love without Love

Love is God no doubt unseen
But omnipresent to look in
Love no eyes to see any sin
Makes one forsee clean
Fans involve in aweful din
Still induces game to win.
Love has no ears to hear
No mouth to speak dear
Understands every tongue
Sometimes does wrong
No legs to walk along
Exults in dance and song
Love without attraction
Matter of manipulation
Love without kind consent
Remains not truly decent
Chances of making violent
Like unruly mulish student
Love of love in much not enough
Invites loss as such being rough
Love without love a hub of mob
An accursed house makes sob
An unduly fruitless job to rob
Misleading to think it superb

117. Where Comes Inspiration

Inspiration doesn't lie in profound and wealthy possession
Nor in luxury, sophisticated skyscraper construction
Rather in the world of failure or dearth, innovation action
Sweet words, sweet voice, touches every heart in exultation
With miraculous alteration in deeds, thoughts and comprehension.
Unseen the source of inspiration
May come in any way of stimulation
As no football moves unless it is kicked
Inspiration not inspiration if heart is not hurt
But anything that can create a gale inside heart.
Each and every particle in God's beautiful creation
Tiny or huge, living or non-living a source of inspiration
Somebody in some way inspired brings a modification
From a man to moral, common to uncommon perception
From a devil to human, mortality to immortalization.

118. Something Remained Untold

Far away from the world of love being highly immature
Couldn't perceive your body language due to childish nature
Couldn't really comprehend you, that alluring smile
You were not remaining aloof from me even a while
Your posture seemed me the sparkling angel of heaven so merry
Your gait in front of me assumed the dance of celestial fairies
Your presence in the bathing ghats as if coincidental
Thy appearance again and again beyond my imagination oriental
Sitting like a child in the group before me stole my attraction
But never did I bother or take to my mind's calculation
Your eyes gazing at me haunted sometimes I felt
The hidden desire inside you nearing me seen myself melt
In the wee hours often your body dashed against me
Myself ashamed of it and strived to keep me distant
The rapport between you and me made me ignorant
Days after days passed away leaving something untold
That puzzled, disturbed, suffered and deferred me bold.
Often I guessed how you created opportunity to meet me
Fear and sameness battled my mind being gloomy.
Dared not to talk to you in inevitable fright
Dare not to touch you though chance to invite
The day when I came to know you fell in love
It was high time to taste the fruits of joyous love.
I wish the day would come back with a last chance

Had not at all lost that joy of divine romance.

119. Too Much

How painful loneliness one can realize once deserted
By the sea attachment out of too much of love vested
When love hosted by love unrequited
Force of love forced to be dived and far shifted to solidarity
Deserted island of love starts aching afflicted with intensity
When love becomes cheap it kills your humanity
Too much of wealth snatches away sound sleep
Nights shrinked to pervade the bed to dream
Pensive mood sarcastically laughs at you to scream.
Too much of dreams plunge into the ocean of fantasy
Heart coaxed with masked ecstasy
Third eye falls asleep in the lap of fancy
Too much of land remains untrodden and ignored
One's own range of crime
Dominantly abhorred
Decreases the life span inside the cage of severity entangled
Too much of pamper makes one hamper
The trend of obedience, cutting the sphere of temper
Depth of closeness packed with chaotic wrapper
Too much of attachment detached far away
The lover and the beloved never crossing parallel way
Till the end in the air they sway
Too much of love make one more blind to see
The unreality before him seems enforcing reality
As if soared in vacuum with no reach of vicinity.

Too much of belief steal away your confidence
From yourself to you dispelling thought-provoking prudence
The essence of life hijacked by the power of solitariness
Too much of hope disheartens the consequence
Heartbroken, mind squeezed in frequence of vehemence
Eminence lost in the absence of credence

120. Life A Long Sentence

Life is a long sentence having some punctuation
Keeps one going on to tackle all types of situations
Comma, one after the other, adds the name of life's events
Semi colon continues the movement
Brackets preserve the alternatives for need
If we are short fall of any deed
Full stop does not end the journey of life
Rather forces to a new beginning deleting strife
If there's no question, no answer comes from minds mill
Underlying truth of life, question mark can reveal
Apostrophe claims for own possession with legal rights
Letting no-one to encroach with might
Inverted commas surround the originality to highlight
Life without punctuations makes one obscure to cite.

9 798885 464918

Printed by Libri Plureos GmbH in Hamburg,
Germany